In *The Chief Growth Officer's Manifesto*, Allen D'Angelo advises us that the pursuit for growth is best achieved when it is grounded in a "process for growth".

Allen's guidance for growth is clearly laid out in this manifesto. Using these principles has resulted in significant growth in my business.

By placing a process for growth into the planning and, by extension, the culture of your business, and by establishing the strategies in this fine book with your managers and decision makers, abundant opportunities will be discovered. You will find a methodology herein, to weigh and position these newly found opportunities for meaningful growth for your business. As this process for growth becomes a part of your company's culture, it can become an effective tool (and competitive advantage) for leaders to have at the ready—skilled growth-minded managers and team members.

DAVID RIPIANZI, PRESIDENT
YMAA PUBLICATION CENTER, INC.

This is the first book I recommend to any leader who asks the secret to success in this business. In *The Chief Growth Officer's Manifesto,* Allen D'Angelo M.S reveals the seven core growth strategies seasoned business leaders must articulate in their business to mobilize their teams and help them realize the ultimate vision of leadership.

FRED SULLIVAN, VICE-PRESIDENT
AQUATITE INNOVATIVE SOLUTIONS

THE
CHIEF
GROWTH
OFFICER'S
MANIFESTO

WHY EVERY BUSINESS LEADER
MUST THINK LIKE A
CHIEF GROWTH OFFICER

ALLEN R. D'ANGELO, M.S.

Published by Archer Ellison Publishing Company,
A division of Archer Ellison, Inc.
7025 CR 46A, #1071
Lake Mary, FL 32746
Phone: 800-449-4095 • Email: archer@archerellison.com

Hardcover ISBN: 978-1-57472-704-3
Paperback ISBN: 978-1-57472-703-6

For more information about the marketing and speaking services of Allen R. D'Angelo, please contact the publisher via the contact information above.

Printed in the United States of America

Dedication

This book is dedicated to my father, Robert D'Angelo, and my mother, Annette D'Angelo, for teaching me many important life and business lessons.

It is from you I learned the life-lesson of 'never giving up.' I feel… your example inspired me from the early foundations of my life in our small New England community—to watching your successful career in the field of engineering sales expand. I felt… empowered through each lesson you taught me. I will never forget the lesson of 'creating value' for others. Thank you, Dad, for telling me how proud you were of me during our weekly visits together. I heard you loud and clear in each of those moments. Remembrances of your kind interactions with people from all walks of life and all the lessons you taught me growing up still abound in me daily—and will continue to guide me throughout my journey in life. I found… unconditional support and love you both gave so freely. You have helped me build a strong foundation of confidence early on, which sustains me to this very day. Thoughts of you both and the many adventures we once shared will continue to provide a daily dose of inspiration to me. Thank you.

Contents

Acknowledgments

I have written this book with a significant sense of urgency and personal commitment. Many business leaders, chief executive officers (CEOs) chief growth officers (CGOs), and chief marketing officers (CMOs) are struggling to understand and agree upon the roles and pathways that lead the company to attain organic growth.

This book presents the seven principles of organic growth that all business leaders, especially CEOs, CMOs, CGOs and their corporate managers, must know to successfully grow their organizations.
This is a book about strategy, understanding, and communication that leads to implementation. I have dedicated my career to studying, consulting and implementing the principles of organic growth with clients for the past two decades.

Many people have contributed their time, energy, wisdom, skills, and support to this book and I would like to thank all of them collectively at this time.

In addition, I wish to acknowledge David Ripianzi, President of YMAA Publication Center, Inc., for bringing a kindred-spirit, valuable insights, friendship and thoughtful commentary to important points in the narrative of this book and throughout our rewarding work together over the past five years.

My thanks to Cynthia Khan, Regional Vice-President, US & Canada, Strategic Alliances at Salesforce for her encouragement one year ago today as we talked together about the principles in this book during her long but enjoyable commute home.

I wish to extend a special thank you to Matthew Mocorro, Chief Marketing Officer at Market Traders Institute, Inc., an Inc. 5000 company, for his support, advice, directional comments and inspiration in writing this book.

I am appreciative of the support of Brian Rix, President, and Fred Sullivan, Vice-President of AquaTITE Innovative Solutions for their review of this book and I wish them continued success in applying the principles found throughout this book to their growing company.

I am grateful for the work of Kimberly Fields, for her tireless, persistent and consistent work in editing this published work.

I wish to give a very special thank you with much gratitude to Kim Leonard for her work on the design of this book as well as her ceaseless encouragement and support.

I would like to thank Dr. Leonard Berry, Professor Emeritus of Texas A&M University for his close mentorship and personal support throughout my study of services marketing at university and during the early development of my strategic consulting practice.

Foreword

What characteristics do certain business leaders possess that make them significantly more effective at growing companies than others, against the prevailing economic headwinds of the moment?

It is time for business leaders, especially chief executive officers (CEOs), chief marketing officers (CMOs), chief growth officers (CGOs) and their corporate teams to think more clearly about how they will come together to make teams more effective at creating organic growth. Many are facing significant headwinds of resistance in growing their companies within their present ecosystems.

Whether your company has incorporated the role of a chief growth officer as a corporate leader now, or not, is not important. What is important is that every member of the corporate center of your organization unites around the important principles of growth presented in each chapter of this book.

In this book two important questions are raised and answered:

> How should members of the corporate center, business leaders and division managers form common expectations about the growth?

> How should leaders form a shared corporate vision for growth that is articulated cogently to all in the company?

Unfortunately these questions are not asked enough in corporate settings, nor are they discussed in a meaningful way by many companies. This book aims to change this by raising the seven most important issues, one per chapter, for the purpose of centering leadership and the whole company around growth.

It is my hope that the principles presented in *The Chief Growth Officer's Manifesto* will influence a positive chain-reaction among business leaders.

Organic growth involves more than making improvements in marketing, or selling—applying the principles herein to the business is more complex and involved than most leaders may first realize.

The organic growth principles in *The Chief Growth Officer's Manifesto* seek to influence leaders to focus team members around a new way of thinking, talking and acting together.

The growth-minded executive will use the principles herein in refocusing the company's portfolio strategy, for properly funding organic growth, harmonizing technology with sales and marketing measures, agreeing on growth goals, and putting a precise accountability system in place to create sustainable and purposeful growth.

With the principles in *The Chief Growth Officer's Manifesto*, executive leaders will expand the growth capacity of the company to triumph over the prevailing headwinds of economic resistance they face now, and in the future.

Introduction

When companies with a history of positive organic growth become challenged to grow in some way the chief marketing officer (CMO) is often the first to be put on the firing line. A study from Accenture Strategy reveals that as many as half of chief executive officers (CEOs) view CMOs as the primary driver of growth in a company. That same study indicates 37 percent of CEOs would not hesitate to put CMOs on the firing line first. According to the study, chief sales officers and chief strategy officers were next in the line of fire.

CEOs of companies in the midst of a transformation may no longer be likely to simply accept slower growth as an inevitable sign that their businesses have matured. Instead, many CEOs are looking to technology, innovation and sustainability to find new growth.

During the writing of this book, the Coca-Cola Company decided to replace the CMO role with a chief growth officer (CGO) as it moves its brand focus from a classic beverage company to a technology-focused company. As Marcos de Quinto retires from his role as CMO, Coca-Cola is merging marketing with customer and commercial teams, creating the new CGO role, which will be held by Francisco Crespo.

The restructuring of Coca-Cola is focused on transforming the company into a "growth-oriented and consumer-centered" beverage company, according to the company.

Other consumer goods companies have hired CGOs recently. Coty, Mondeléz and Colgate-Palmolive have hired CGOs to "accelerate growth efforts" and "bring focus and growth" to their platforms. Fast-moving consumer goods were the first to appoint CGOs, beginning half a decade ago, with Coca-Cola as the latest to do so.

Historically, as companies have matured, CEOs cease looking internally for growth. Instead of growing organically, they grow their topline inorganically by acquiring smaller companies, or seek transformative acquisitions of high-growth companies.

Past research suggests that companies realize enough cost savings to cover the premium paid in only thirty-six percent of acquisitions. Most companies do not realize enough cost savings to cover the premium paid. In the other sixty-four percent, total annual shareholder returns average a negative two-percent.

One Booz & Company research study suggests that investors can distinguish between companies that have realized significant organic disruptive growth through acquisitions from those that have merely gotten larger after the acquisition occurs.

Future CEOs, CGOs and CMOs in merging companies, must face the music and work out how their companies will generate stronger organic growth after the acquisition.

Is this trend in hiring CGOs, a sign that CEOs are becoming wary of the CMO's ability to drive growth?

Will marketing lose the boardroom seat, instead reporting to the new CGO?

If marketers continue to position themselves as experts in "brand positioning, digital fads, millennials, and advertising," more CMO positions may be headed for the firing lines in the future.

The coming era of the CGO will cause marketers to break from formulaic thinking of the past in which they rely on templates of past successes as the basis for ideas.

In the age of the CGO, marketers must focus on performance, become more data-driven, and bring transformational thinking to marketing.

As CMOs face greater pressure to report revenues in an increasingly digital advertising environment the shuffling of the deck in marketing will bring forceful, but positive change for making CMOs more accountable marketers in the future.

The purpose of the *The Chief Growth Officer's Manifesto* is to stimulate growth-minded conversations by empowering readers to bring structured and principled thought leadership to their companies with clear and measurable objectives.

Prologue

I have written this book with a significant sense of urgency and personal commitment. Many business leaders, chief executive officers (CEOs) chief growth officers (CGOs), and chief marketing officers (CMOs) are rethinking the role marketing, strategy and growth-mindedness play in the organization.

In companies today many executives, including CMOs are facing extraordinary pressure. In certain cases the stress has led to higher executive turnover. A few companies have eliminated the role of CMOs altogether, replacing them instead with executives who function as CGOs.

Many business leaders are not sure how to properly address the subject of managing organic growth and some are not even trying to improve. Business leaders should and must strive to do better. Much is at stake in this competitive global economy.

Through the concepts in this book business leaders and the business community at large are nurturing and funding growth-forward thinking in new ways inside their organizations. Companies of all sizes are finding new ways to bring greater balance and certainty to their organizations using these practical and proactive decision-making approaches to organic growth.

Each chapter in this book presents an important core competency of the chief growth officer that should be utilized by every business leader. Many CEOs are using this book to guide implementation-focused discussions at weekly meetings and effectively influencing each business leader on their team to think like a chief growth officer.

1

Use a Growth Proposition to Lead with a Compelling Vision for Growth

Everyone in your company needs to have a clear vision of the future that compels and inspires them to contribute to the forward motion of the business. One particularly valuable skill growth-focused leaders must possess is the ability to translate important challenges facing the organization into a cohesive strategy for harvesting the company's best opportunities for growth.

Yes, the best leaders impart a sense of enthusiasm about their vision of the future. However, the very best leaders understand that their vision provides the necessary direction for reaching the prize. By articulating how and why the team must pursue something much greater for the future than can be seen today, growth leaders provide the fuel that runs the engine.

This chapter is about guiding you as the growth leader—the Chief Growth Officer (CGO) of your company—in creating a dynamic and clear statement of a compelling vision for growing the business. As a growth leader you must provide crisp communication about your expected high-level outcomes, driven by perpetual persistence and intentionality. You must empower your teams to push through the inevitable obstacles they must face in achieving growth.

To accomplish this, we will look at the importance of leading with a powerful and impactful growth proposition, which allows you to transfer a strong sense of the vision to your teams.

The Growth Proposition is a clear statement of strategy and action. It summarizes a specific overall growth target of the company; *why* the company is dedicated to reaching this growth target, *how* it will achieve this growth. It is written to inspire and instill a strong sense of certainty the achievement of the growth target is within reach.

We will see clear examples demonstrating the characteristics of a good growth proposition, and discuss the value of creating yours.

THE IMPORTANCE OF DEVELOPING A POWERFUL AND IMPACTFUL GROWTH PROPOSITION FOR IMPARTING A VISION FOR GROWTH

Your growth proposition provides the foundation to ensure the psychology of healthful growth becomes a habit inside your company at all levels. This ensures that the important components of your vision for growth are constantly in front of *everyone* in your company.

James Allen once said, "*Dream lofty dreams, and as you dream, so shall you become. Your vision is the promise of what you shall one day be; Your ideal is the prophecy of what you shall at last unveil.*"

Each person in your company may have a different understanding of the vision the company should pursue. Until the Chief Growth Officer (CGO) develops the formal statement of the growth vision in the form of the growth proposition, the collective mind of the company may be a rudderless ship at sea.

Developing the growth proposition is paramount because in many organizations the challenge is that there is not a large enough vision to inspire relentless growth. Wimpy and small visions have no power to stir the blood of those who must work to attain great success in the pursuit of growth.

The growth proposition must answer the question: "Why is reaching this growth target so important to us as a *team*?"

Simply stated, most people will do more for others than they ever will do for themselves. To be effective, the growth proposition must identify the people you want to impact most—your fellow workers and your customers.

Reasons come first, the growth comes second.

> *"Dream no small dreams;*
> *For these have no power to*
> *move the hearts of men."*
> **—JOHANN WOLFGANG VON GOETHE—**

Finally, the growth proposition fosters a sense of positive expectancy and sets the stage for the development of the proper attitude and atmosphere for growth throughout the organization. When there is the foundation of a positive mental attitude toward growth, the sense of the drudgery of pushing toward company goals changes to the sense of the team being pulled effortlessly toward the higher altitude of the desired growth target.

GUIDELINES FOR DEVELOPING
THE GROWTH PROPOSITION

First, the Growth Proposition should articulate the specific results the company is expected to derive from its growth initiatives. This must be expressed as a specific measure; for example, as an increase in the number of customers, revenues and/or profits. The measure should be expressed over two or more comparable periods of time.

Second, the Growth Proposition should describe the benefits customers and employees should expect from the growth initiatives the company is dedicated to embracing and investing in.

Third, the Growth Proposition should mention how each of the operating units, product lines, service categories, proposed initiatives, or other divisions of the business will contribute to the growth. If key divisions of the business will not contribute to the overall growth of the company, this should be addressed in a balanced way in the growth proposition as well.

Last, the Growth Proposition should be written to motivate, challenge, stimulate, and provide certainty that the team is capable of achieving the growth target. It should reflect the culture and style of the company as a whole. It should reflect the direction that has been set by leadership and align with the overall mission of the company.

Some Chief Growth Officers find it helpful to include key descriptive words that foster variety in the growth proposition, as well as convey a strong sense of certainty:

Examples of words that add color and variety to the written growth proposition include:

expansion	adventure	rapidity
acceleration	bold	challenge
excitement	preeminence	

Examples of words that add stability and certainty to the written growth proposition include:

protection	predictability	confidence
safety	security	inevitability
sustainability	assurance	

Simple Example of a Growth Proposition for a File Sharing Software Company

Our company is dedicated to accepting our new competitive challenge to zoom ahead to become the market leader in online cloud storage for the trust and succession niche this year. We will increase topline sales from $56 million at the end of this fiscal year (20xx) to $85 million by the end of next fiscal year (20xx).

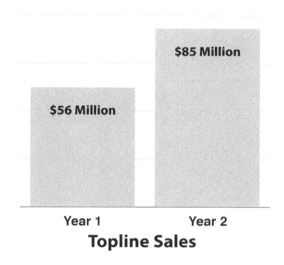

$85 Million

$56 Million

Year 1   Year 2

Topline Sales

This will be achieved by increasing our customer base by 10% (Growth Opportunity Bar #1); increasing the average ticket value of our customers by 15% (Growth Opportunity Bar #2); increasing the average customer frequency of purchase by 20% (Growth Opportunity Bar #3) — over the course of the next fiscal year.

This growth will provide us with greater predictability related to scale, allowing us to fund a new, more secure data center,

Growth Target End of the Next Fiscal Year by Growth Rate:

Increase Customer Base	X	Increase Average Ticket Value	X	Increase Frequency of Purchase	=	Growth
1.10	X	1.15	X	1.20	=	1.52

GROWTH TARGET IS: 52%

Growth Target End of the Next Fiscal Year By Dollars:*

$56 Million	**Sales This Year**
X 1.10	Customer Base Growth Rate
$62 Million	**Growth Opportunity Bar #1**
X 1.15	Average Ticket Growth Rate
$71 Million	**Growth Opportunity Bar #2**
X 1.20	Frequency of Purchase Growth Rate
$85 Million	**Growth Opportunity Bar #3**

GROWTH TARGET IS: $85 Million

* Here each Growth Opportunity Bar reflects the highest-yielding projected results of the best growth initiatives the company has identified in each area of the business that can be achieved by the end of the next fiscal year.

adding six new job positions and giving our customers faster data uptake rates and greater data safety. In addition, we will give customers unlimited storage on an unlimited number of devices.

Breakdown of Operating Unit Contribution to Growth

Consumer Division: We will add online marketing and strategic partnerships that will drive an increase in consumer sales by 3% by the end of the year. The addition of three more consumer, higher-priced product lines will have the effect of boosting consumer ticket values by 7%, causing consumers who buy from our competitors to become shifters by buying our new offerings. We will add a monthly recurring revenue billing option for increasing the frequency of purchase by a factor of 1.3 times current levels across the consumer business.

Business Division: We will add three top national law office client-intensive network contracts to our business, which will increase the topline revenue by 7% by the end of the year. The addition of two more higher-priced business product lines will have the effect of boosting ticket values by 3%. We will install a monthly recurring revenue billing option. Post-installation, the new revenue system will effortlessly increase the frequency of purchase by a factor of 1.4 times current levels across the business division.

Our biggest competitor, Company XYZ, is projected to finish this year with topline revenue of $60 million. We know that Company XYZ is two years away from building a much-needed data center. We know our market of aging Baby Boomers is growing at 20% per year with their need for trust development and easy secure storage of electronic documents for their estates. As a result of these factors and our strength in planning our data storage build out, we have a distinctive advantage to become the market leader by the end of this year (20xx).

We embrace our above growth strategy as an adventure of the highest magnitude possible and the best way to continue to add innovation and high value for our consumer and business customers.

THE VALUE OF THE GROWTH PROPOSITION

The growth proposition allows the company to maintain a higher level of visibility, accountability and accuracy about its growth in important ways.

The growth proposition unites the corporate center around one central vision that can more easily be shared and broken down into digestible portions for operating unit managers and their teams.

When the company properly funds growth, and cost controls are correctly in place, the growth proposition contributes to creating the success cycle. When the growth proposition is correct and strong, if there are other weakening factors such as poor delivery, or a lack of quality of implementation, growth will be affected. Comparing implementation across a well-articulated and detailed growth proposition will show where the breakdown is occurring when measuring the actual performance of each of the operating units and their initiatives.

The growth proposition provides the foundation for developing a new language about growth for the company. This can be used to hold more meaningful conversations about where to look for additional future growth opportunities with operating unit managers.

The growth proposition provides the way to gain and build growth momentum in an upward spiral. When the team clearly envisions the way to success, the more they find new ways to further succeed. Belief in the potential of the growth proposition drives implementation. Implementation yields results, which reinforces the belief in the potential, which in turn drives higher levels of implementation.

Use your growth proposition to lead. Use it to impart a vivid, stimulating and compelling vision for growth that empowers everyone in the company to believe in your higher causal purpose. Use your growth proposition to indoctrinate your people and your customers to fully believe so strongly in your vision for their future that they cannot possibly imagine a future without the vision coming to fruition.

2

Create a Common
Language for Growth

As a Chief Growth Officer with your Growth Proposition fully in place, you embrace your role like the navigator of a great ship—your organization. You see before you a vast ocean filled with hidden treasures that no one else sees below the cresting waters.

You see new opportunities, overlooked markets, strategic relationships, transactions and areas for collaborative partnerships that are there for your team to access. You actively seek the thrill of this great adventure.

In leading this new direction of your journey, you are in pursuit of manifesting a bigger and bolder vision for your company, to arrive at your new destiny of organic growth.

You are always striving to improve the skills of your craft. Your primary tool will be your Growth Proposition. As you communicate with your team, your chief aim is to empower everyone to see the vision and mobilize them to take the actions that lead to tapping these exciting new sources of organic growth.

You know that if the rigging of your ship is to be properly drawn and the rudder of your ship is to lead you to your desired destination, that your crew must not only be on board, they must be fully engaged for delivering their utmost during every mile on this journey.

It behooves you to develop a proper commanding language for each phase along your journey to your growth target. This empowers everyone in the corporate center, as well as your teams, to know how to communicate about growth together.

> *"One should use common words*
> *to say uncommon things."*
> **— ARTHUR SCHOPENHAUER —**

Everyone has his or her own language. As Chief Growth Officer, you are leading a subculture of talented team members. It is in keeping with this wisdom that you should have a common language for discussing the highly distinctive growth issues your company faces.

Certainly, when Chief Growth Officers use identifying language, it creates a sense of insider knowledge, bonding, and belonging. Beyond this, your "secret growth language" is one that will be unique to your organization. It will define the precise nature of the organic growth that is sought and where it is likely to be found so that all team members may clearly recognize and always pursue the best opportunities.

In this chapter, we will consider the importance of creating common language expressions for growth and the keys to ponder when constructing them, with clear examples demonstrating the characteristics of a succinct organic growth language glossary.

WHY CONSTRUCTING A UNIQUE COMMON GROWTH LANGUAGE IS ESSENTIAL FOR SUCCESS

The development of a common, globally understood and frequently used lexicon for organic growth eliminates unnecessary redundancies, saves time and money, and fosters better communication among your teams.

Just as each person in the company may think differently about growth initially, every individual will have their own way of talking about organic growth, as well. This naturally occurring inefficiency is one the Chief Growth Officer cannot afford to allow to continue for very long.

Until the Chief Growth Officer deliberately installs the proper growth phraseology, there may very well be fewer meaningful conversations about important growth issues than there should be. With a lack of communication, or miscommunication, we find overlapping initiatives, wasted effort, and unproductive investment, quite possibly in important areas of the business.

With a written and shared list of important growth terms in place, clarity arrives and confusion dissipates. Effective growth leaders use a unique growth language to inspire people to communicate about growth issues in the best way possible and that resonates throughout the organization, as well.

The topic of growth achievement is by nature more esoteric and difficult to contemplate. When great leaders choose an empowering growth language, they give everyone in the company a way to discuss how to think about important change issues for spurring advancement. The use of a common growth language becomes more valuable to the company as the team looks for relevant ways to fulfill the Growth Proposition through growth initiatives.

The development of a growth language can be a good step in enabling the company to think differently about regaining lost growth and profitability.

Finally, a common growth language reduces employee resistance by creating a diverting focal point that moves people *away* from points of confrontation, and *toward* a uniting goal whereby leaders may then advance conversations about organic growth.

THE USE OF A COMMON GROWTH LANGUAGE IN ACTION

To understand the power of a consistent growth language, consider the story of a company that was modernizing its technology. It wanted all employees to focus on how changes would be received by the firm's customers, and by extension, how those changes would affect the company's ability to grow organically and profitably.

Corporate leaders faced substantial resistance from the company's employees, however, who believed that they were already producing the world's best product.

To break the stalemate, the smart CGO introduced the team to a new growth phrase; "relative customer value." Here the term "relative customer value" is defined as the extra value the customer receives from the implementation of a growth initiative. This term gave everyone a way to discuss how to best modernize the company and led to some positive changes among the employees that had been seemingly impossible to convert to the new technology.

In this case, customers were so delighted by the change that many became more loyal to the company and the brand.

Having a common term for thinking and talking about growth really helped everyone in the company get on the same page and clarify what was important as they looked for new coherent ways to grow the business.

As the above story shows, just one powerful common growth term or phrase can create buy-in from employees in an important way. Having a common terminology for growth brings positive thought-leadership and more enlightening conversations to the table to engage employees better, differently.

Additionally, distributing a company-wide glossary of common growth language terms makes your employees' jobs easier. When employees are on the front lines, they will rely on a small number of focused terms from the growth language to guide key decisions that drive organic growth.

GUIDELINES FOR CONSTRUCTING A COMMON GROWTH LANGUAGE

The growth terms and definitions should be organized in the form of a formal written *Organic Growth Glossary* in order to formally establish the company's organic growth language.

The growth language glossary provides a formal list of focused growth terms followed by a formal statement of the meaning, or significance of the term, phrase, or idiom as related to organic growth.

The terms related to your organic growth language may, at a first glance by your reader, appear to be easily understandable. However, due to the multi-ordinate nature of commonly used words, when some defining words are combined together to form the organic growth term, they take on an entirely different, often idiomatic meaning. Because of this, growth-related terms must always have very clear accompanying definitions.

Most importantly, the development of a growth language should include terms selected to reflect the *important measures*, and *actionable contributions*, that have been identified in the Growth Proposition.

From the example in the sample Growth Proposition from the previous chapter for the cloud storage company, the term *headroom for growth* and the term *shifters* (referenced as customer shifting from buying the offerings of our competitors to buying our offerings) are good examples of measurable and actionable organic growth terms. These terms were clearly defined in the "Growth Glossary" of the company.

Growth language terms almost always point to or lead to organic growth opportunities. It is important for the Chief Growth Officer to provide a clear definition of the best "organic growth opportunity" for the company.

Example of a clear definition for guiding an organic growth opportunity

This example is for Manitowoc, a company that owns one business in heavy-lifting cranes and another in commercial equipment for the food service industry:

Organic Growth Opportunity Definition of Manitowoc: The best new opportunity will be favorable to both the heavy-lifting business and the food services business by providing shared economies of scale and yielding a minimum of $250 million in market sales within 16 months of start date.

The team at Manitowoc accepted this challenge by conducting extensive research. The best growth opportunity for both businesses turned out to be in emerging markets, where local expertise is critical and managerial talent is scarce. With this research in hand, Manitowoc growth leadership mandated that emerging market expertise was critical for all corporate functions—a move that gives the two businesses access to a capability that neither could develop nearly as well on it own. The two businesses share common challenges, such as understanding customs. Together they also provide access to larger opportunities, such as making presentations to authorities looking for direct investment in their countries.

The organic growth language should enable the Chief Growth Officer to help each operating unit identify its growth opportunities and decide how to best realize them.

EXAMPLE OF A CLEAR ORGANIC GROWTH LANGUAGE GLOSSARY:

Organic Growth Glossary for the XYZ Corporation

Headroom for Growth: The business we do not presently have minus the business we are unlikely to obtain.

Net LTV Margin: The difference between our cost per acquisition (CPA) of a customer and the lifetime value (LTV) of a customer.

For example, a digital advertising opportunity is more attractive when the cost to acquire a customer hits the right target (not always the least costly) and where the customer delivers a higher lifetime buying value. The higher this margin is, the better a campaign is performing.

Shifters: Clients who shift between two or more suppliers, or would shift their business to our company if they discovered a better offering.

Wants-Offer Margin: The difference between what clients receive from their current supplier(s) and what else they want or need that would cause them to buy from our company.

Up-Buy: Encouraging clients to upgrade their purchase to a superior version of our product or service, because they receive extra value in doing so. This term describes customer "pull" behavior and is in contrast to Up-Sell, which reflects a "push" behavior.

Opportunity Bar Gap: The difference between the highest yielding potential opportunities available to our company, compared to the average or lowest yielding opportunities. The idea is to get unit managers to identify and justify the highest and best potential opportunities so that they are less likely to propose investing in areas that will yield only average, or smaller than optimal, wins.

ADOPT AND DIFFUSE YOUR GLOSSARY

Once the Chief Growth Officer, in cooperation with the corporate center, has thoughtfully developed and approved the best possible growth glossary, it is time to adopt and diffuse this lexicon throughout the company, starting with the C-suite and other leadership. The organic growth glossary is then adopted throughout the operating units.

The establishment and adoption of a company-wide language for growth greatly improves the value of performance-based conversations in which leaders are checking in with unit managers.

Instead of the CEO asking common questions, the corporate organic growth glossary changes the line of questioning. With the organic growth glossary firmly in place, the growth leader can now also ask questions focused more on capturing new opportunities for growth:

Before the Common Growth Language Questions	After the Common Growth Language Questions
How are you doing against your goals?	Where is our best future *Headroom for Growth* opportunity?
What's our customer attrition rate?	What are our biggest *Wants-Offer Margin* opportunities for recapturing lost clients?

What are you doing to bring in new clients and orders?	Who are our most likely *Shifters*?
How can we become more productive?	Which of our digital advertising inventory providers is delivering the thickest *Net LTV Margin*?
What are you doing to sell more of our products per month?	What do our high-end customers want, that we're not presently offering, that would get them to invest more with us? (*Opportunity Bar Gap*)

When the Chief Growth Officer leads the organization to develop a clear language for growth, managers will be less likely to overestimate growth potential, which creates inefficiencies, and more likely to develop focused initiatives, with higher-performing conduits of opportunities.

3

Clarify Your Core Growth Target

For the Chief Growth Officer, like a former decathlon gold medalist who is coming back to beat her own former javelin world record distance score, the competition and the pressure to perform can be fierce.

The gold medalist battles not only her current competitors, but also her most fierce nemesis, herself. She is determined to pour blood, sweat and every ounce of energy into breaking her own past world record.

To win the gold and break that record, she must run, gain maximum momentum, and then with perfect timing, throw the eight-foot, two-inch spear farther than any human ever has before in this role.

She must throw that javelin the full distance to reach the target goal, or she will walk away in defeat.

Just like the gold medalist, the Chief Growth Officer and his team must have the right growth target completely locked in before momentum can be gained.

Choosing the right growth target spells the difference between success and failure. The target will become the core focal point that all efforts, work and initiatives of the team drive toward.

In this chapter, we will look at how one newly hired Chief Growth Officer brought in a new perspective to an Inc. 5000 company to solve a fundamental growth problem by providing a clear growth target. We will look at two perspectives for setting a proper growth target, followed by questions to consider when doing so.

JOHN'S STORY

It was against the backdrop of conflict and competing interests amidst raging factions that this unique Inc. 5000 technology firm hired Chief Growth Officer John Billings.

The company had four operating units. The CEO had been pushing too hard, overreaching in two favored operating units that were thought of as the growth engines for the company.

John highlighted how the company had stopped investing in the headroom for growth in two of its operating units. He pointed out that the company overinvested in the two other operating units, which had become "favorite children" of the company. Had the overall growth target of the company been set properly first, then the performance contribution of each operating unit would have been measured against its overall potential for growth.

John explained that as a result of these problems, the company wasted investment dollars and added unnecessary costs that were not generating a sufficient return. Money was then diverted away from the two "less favored" operating units of the company, which became starved for investment dollars, causing foregone and missed opportunities to multiply. Innovation withered, causing organic growth initiatives to atrophy, further resulting in a kind of anorexia in these operating units (next page, top).

John proposed a new balanced approach for setting more realistic growth targets that considered the *headroom for growth* of the company as a whole, properly fed all operating units the resources they needed, and adjusted the growth performance contribution expectation of each unit to a realistic and reachable level (next page, bottom). John's subsequent plan to align the less favored operating units proposed an additional 148% growth—taking the company from $306 million in sales to $451 million in sales.

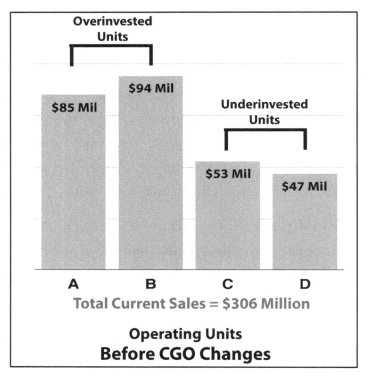

Overinvested Units

$85 Mil

$94 Mil

Underinvested Units

$53 Mil

$47 Mil

A   B   C   D

Total Current Sales = $306 Million

Operating Units
Before CGO Changes

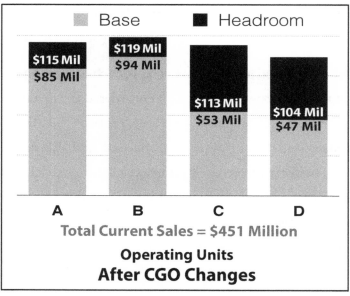

Base   Headroom

$115 Mil
$85 Mil

$119 Mil
$94 Mil

$113 Mil
$53 Mil

$104 Mil
$47 Mil

A   B   C   D

Total Current Sales = $451 Million

Operating Units
After CGO Changes

TWO PERSPECTIVES ON SETTING A GROWTH TARGET

There are two ways to think about setting a growth target: -a *Market Back* perspective and a *Headroom for Growth* perspective.

Market Back Perspective

With a *Market Back* perspective, you create a point of view. You determine what the natural growth rates are for the markets you compete in. Then, you choose some increment above or below the market growth rate, factoring in a reasonable relative improvement to your company's current rate of growth and select that as the right growth target. This is one way to obtain the point of view for determining your growth target.

Natural Growth Rate	X	Reasonable Improvement Rate	=	Growth Target
10%	X	15%	=	11.5%

MARKET BACK GROWTH TARGET IS: 11.5%

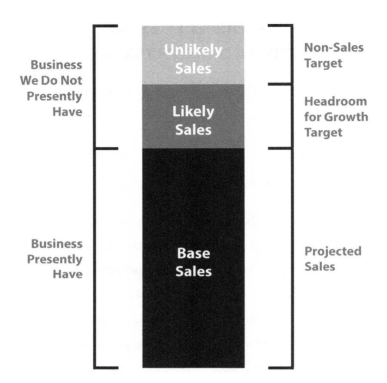

Base Sales and Headroom Breakdown

Business We Do Not Presently Have		Business We Are Unlikely to Obtain		Headroom for Growth Target
	X		=	
$100 Million	X	$85 Million	=	$15 Million

HEADROOM FOR GROWTH IS: $15 MILLION

Headroom for Growth Perspective

As you recall from the last chapter, I defined *Headroom for Growth* as the business we do not currently have, minus the business we are unlikely to get (see opposite).

It is important that corporate growth leaders investigate all of the nuances and subtleties around their headroom, but for most, especially those starting on this journey, this is a pretty good placeholder.

After some investigative research is conducted, business intelligence is gathered, the data scientists are called in, and perhaps after discussions between CEO and CGO have taken place, a true, clarified picture of your headroom for growth emerges.

With that clarified picture of the headroom for your business, you are free to focus on what investments may need to be made to increase capacity, add in more capabilities, or gather resources to capture the headroom you have identified.

There must be an investment to increase or add capabilities; if you had them before now, you would have already acquired the headroom and the revenues. *There is always a required investment to be made to extend or add proficiencies to the business.*

Investment Example

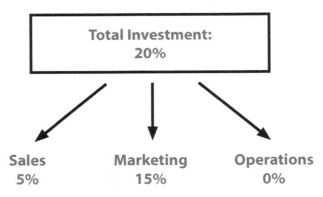

Ask yourself, as a corporate growth leader, "What kind of an investment can we make?" The answer to this question tells you how much headroom you think you can capture over a certain time frame. You can derive the right growth target from this with fellow leaders through a moderate discussion.

Using the headroom method, you start with a clear focus on your growth potential, and then you descend your targets from that, as opposed to the other way around.

Once you have derived your growth target, as we will see in a later chapter, you will figure out ways to fund this growth for free; this will be done collaboratively with your team.

THE LARGE MERCHANDISE
RETAILER

Now, we will look at a large merchandise retailer with one thousand initiatives in play, as an example. This retailer is struggling to obtain same store sales growth, which in their business, is what true organic growth really means. They are obsessed with driving more same store sales growth. They are driven to invest, to put those one thousand initiatives behind them.

Then, we ask, where is the true headroom for growth? Is it in driving more foot traffic, getting more people to walk into the stores? Is the true headroom realized by getting patrons to cross the aisle, meaning if they are buying clothing from the store, we influence them to go to electronics and buy a television from the store? Or is the real headroom found amidst people who are already shopping for groceries, or electronics, or clothing, to buy more of those products from you than they are from competitors?

For this retailer, it turned out that although they were obsessively focused on influencing more patrons to walk into the store, and then to cross the aisle, it turned out that actually influencing patrons to buy more in their categories was what delivered the true growth headroom. Simply said, it was easier for this retailer to influence people to buy more

Headroom For Growth For Large Merchandise Retailer

Initiatives Implemented

	Get More Patrons to Walk into Store to Buy	Get In-Store Patrons to Buy More By Crossing the Aisle	Get In-Store Patrons to Buy More In-Category
Data Before Initiative	2,565	4,134	4,315
Data After Initiative	2,614	4,291	4,638
Change	+1.019	+1.038	+1.075
	↑		↑
	Least Likely Obtainable Business		**Most Likely Obtainable Business**

in the categories in which they were already shopping. Attempting to bring more people into the stores turned out to be a much tougher objective to obtain. This was business they were much less likely to get since they were already a very popular retailer.

Out of a thousand initiatives, almost half of them were dedicated to going after growth opportunities they simply didn't have. They reassessed their headroom for growth and transferred many of the resources that were backing the prettier but less tenable opportunities to the ugly duckling initiatives. This created a much better return in funding their new headroom for organic growth.

DEVELOP YOUR GROWTH TARGET PHILOSOPHY.
KNOW WITH CERTAINTY WHY YOU WANT YOUR TEAM TO BE ABOVE AVERAGE, RELATIVE TO THE MARKET

Because growth-focused CEO Jim Kilts of Gillette didn't want his operating divisions to overreach, he held operating units to his philosophy that he wanted them to perform above average, year-in and year-out, relative to the market. To achieve his growth target, he used a Headroom for Growth approach tempered by a Market Back perspective. In Kilts' use of the two approaches, he was determined to strike a purposeful balance. He never wanted team leaders to struggle to get to the top of the pack in any given year. The reason was that striving like this would cause his operating units to overreach, in his view.

Kilts would say, "You never want to strive to be at the top of the pack in any given year. The winner over a five-year period is usually a company that has been in the top third for revenue growth and profitability each year."

In addition, Kilts would explain, "Being number one or two in a given year is not necessarily correlated with industry leadership in the long run. Mr. Kilts, based on research he had commissioned, often said that the quest to occupy top positions in an industry creates a yo-yo effect."

Looking at the data of the Fortune 500 Top Ten Business Rankings, in this current age fraught with issues related to disruption, accessibility to wealth and capital inequality one might disagree with Mr. Kilts, however this depends on how long-run industry leadership is defined.

In the case of Gillette, Mr. Kilts would tone down the inflated targets of his operating managers, not to rein in their ambition; rather, it was to keep them focused on doing the right things at the right times—such as thinking about growth at the bottom of the run of a business cycle, rather than obsessing over growth at the top.

Align your philosophy with your growth target. Maintain congruence. Unite the reason why your growth target is important with a focus on your higher-causal business purpose.

Remember, we are not asking our people to strain or struggle by doing more with less. Instead, we are refocusing them, involving and engaging them in the other initiatives where the potential is greater. Those initiatives are going to get more resources.

The *company* should always do more with less, but should never asking any one *individual* to do more with less. Unfortunately, this happens more often than it should.

This way, leaders help everyone in the company maintain this vital focus on capturing additional growth headroom by fostering a strong belief that progressive ideas, new opportunities and new sources of organic growth are abundant and readily available.

As we will see throughout this book, the implementation of a well-articulated Growth Proposition, the adoption of a focused language for growth, and setting a clear and proper growth target will set the stage for finding new growth opportunities, rethinking the portfolio strategy and discovering creative ways to fund future growth.

QUESTIONS TO ASK WHEN SETTING A GROWTH TARGET:

Market Back Perspective

- What are the naturally occurring growth rates for your industry and how does this compare to your company's growth target?

- What is the right growth target for the company as a whole relative to the current growth rates of the markets you compete in?

- How do you know when you as a leader are overreaching because your company may not be performing better than the market of competitors?

- Do you have a leadership position or new innovation in the marketplace that ensures you will drive higher than market-average growth rates?

- What is your philosophy about wanting to be above average, year in and year out, relative to the market and how does this affect your growth target decisions?

- What is the right growth target for each operating unit of the company?

Headroom for Growth Perspective

- Have you gathered enough business intelligence to understand the nuances of changes impacting growth target decisions that are caused by or that affect your market of customers?

- What does detailed research tell you about the current size and full spectrum of characteristics about your market of customers that are most relevant to your growth target decisions?

- Have you properly applied data science to your research and business intelligence to gain top-down clarity about your ecosystem and how your company and competitors fit into it?

- Have you done enough "on the street" research by talking to actual potential and existing customers to take on their perspectives to gather clues about where additional headroom for growth may be found?

- What is the *headroom for growth* of each of the operating units, or divisions of your company?

- What is the overall *headroom for growth* of your company?

- What is the right growth target for the company as a whole based on the best headroom for growth opportunities?

- What is the right growth target for each operating unit of the company?

- Have you made the intellectual "economic connections" relevant to your growth target necessary to confidently sign-off on unit manager budgets?

- Have you identified and assigned the due diligence initiatives necessary to know with certainty that your growth targets are reachable and likely to be achieved?

- Are there any initiatives that produce less than desirable results for which you could move resources to areas that will contribute better toward reaching the overall growth target? (List the ones to be replaced.)

- How do you know when you are overreaching because there may be less response or more resistance to obtaining the observed growth headroom?

- How do you know when you're not ambitious enough?

- Under what circumstances should you tone down the targets proposed by your operating managers?

- Do you look across operating units to discover opportunities that no unit managers are seeing, or can pursue on their own?

4

Tear Down Walls and Build Bridges to Operating Units

At times, it is important for the Chief Growth Officer to look beyond the technical and analytical aspects of the organization to recognize walls that have been built, or are in the process of being built, and when to erect bridges between siloed departments.

There are social-psychological dimensions to the role that at times require the Chief Growth Officer to adapt their skills in new ways to deal with a silo mentality.

Understanding the conditions that have led to the development of silos within the organization can be a most important and occasionally beguiling, aspect of the work, especially for the new Chief Growth Officer. Such conditions could include: resistance to change, rigid corporate policies that work against effective integrative growth, lingering ideologies of past leaders, or current managers that do not support collaboration.

At times it is important to employ creative ways to eliminate the impact of such sticking points by leveraging programs that remove these walls and build successful bridges from leadership to operating units. Leading such initiatives creates more opportunities for collaboration. Dismantling the walls of the silos between operating units opens pathways to the overall future growth of the company.

In acting as Chief Growth Officer, you always function on two levels.

On one level your aim is to remove obstacles and tear down walls that prevent growth.

Simultaneously, and on a different level, you aim to work with operating units in building bridges. You lead managers to discover for themselves new, underutilized resources and overlooked assets, and to find orders of magnitude growth factors for reaching new heights.

In this chapter, we will focus on two key portfolio management issues the Chief Growth Officer should be equipped to address in managing organic growth:

1. Tearing down the walls, sticking points and problems that develop when operating units become labeled based on past performance.

2. The importance of working with operating managers to actively find new approaches and opportunities for successfully solving complex organic growth problems.

TEAR DOWN WALLS ARISING FROM LABELING OPERATING UNITS

The task of managing organizations is complex. Over the years, consulting groups and experts studying different methods have provided executives with tools for managing the complexities of the organizations we run.

Most corporate leaders with a formal B-school education remember a tool called "The Growth Share Matrix (GSM)."

Originally, GSM was a portfolio-planning model developed by the Boston Consulting Group (BCG) in the 1970s. Today this concept is still taught in a few B-schools. The model served to classify a company's business units based on market share and market growth, relative to the largest competitor.

According to the model (following page), a business unit is labeled as a "Dog," a "Question Mark," a "Cash Cow," or a "Rising Star."

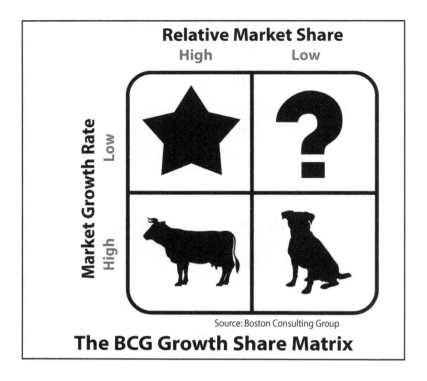

Relative Market Share

High   Low

Market Growth Rate

Low

High

Source: Boston Consulting Group

The BCG Growth Share Matrix

While the GSM was widely used years ago, it has faded in popularity. We have evolved. For example, struggling business units may be generating value for other units that increase monetization in other parts of the company. Focusing on relative market share and market growth out of the context of other driving factors may cause leaders to oversimplify important business decisions.

In today's fast-paced world, we understand why managers like labels. Labels help to simplify complex tasks in managing organizations. Like heuristics, some managers rely on labels to speed up decisions. At least in some cases, the label gives managers a sense of security that they are making good decisions.

In many organizations, the units that are designated as "rising stars" receive the lion's share of investment capital. The other units are viewed as "cash cows" that fund the "rising star" growth engines.

The problem is that these labels define the beliefs about growth, affect operating unit performance, and eventually become self-defeating.

It is better to resist labeling or portfolio stereotyping of units as growth businesses, and instead work with the operating units to create performance results.

If the managers of an operating unit feel solely responsible for the main company's organic growth, they will likely take on more costs and risks than they should.

On the other hand, if an operating unit manager feels that their operating unit is less responsible for driving the growth of the company, they may not be actively requesting, or receiving the resources needed to improve their performance.

It is better that the Chief Growth Officer and Chief Executive Officer think differently about the potential of each unit and work to deliver the necessary resources for each unit to fulfill its potential.

Let's take a look at how CEO Rich Zannino of Dow Jones turned away from labeling and typecasting *The Wall Street Journal*, a struggling "cash cow" operating unit, and chose instead to work with the *Journal* to build a bridge to future growth.

TEARING DOWN TRADITION: *DOW JONES & THE WALL STREET JOURNAL*

Rich Zannino was at the helm as CEO of Dow Jones when one of his operating units, *The Wall Street Journal*, was on a downward slide. The newspaper was not competing well against the flood of online media and it was unappealing to younger readers, whom *The Wall Street Journal's* advertisers coveted.

Zannino and the corporate leadership team at Dow Jones could have sided with the conventional wisdom that newspapers were dying. They could have elected to manage the newspaper rigorously as a "cash cow" operating unit of Dow Jones—cutting costs and reducing reinvestment—using the squeezed profits to fund the growth of Dow's other businesses.

Instead, under the leadership of Rich Zannino, the Dow corporate team worked with *The Wall Street Journal's* management team to revitalize its brand image. They added more entertainment, lifestyle and broadened-interest coverage. They made changes to attract the younger readers their advertisers desired to target. *The Wall Street Journal Weekend Edition* was added to increase readership and advertising opportunities. The result was double-digit organic revenue growth, while the rest of the industry experienced declining revenues. This drove *The Wall Street Journal* to become a national newspaper-of-record, repositioning it to compete with *The New York Times*.

At first, *The Wall Street Journal* teams fought hard against the changes, based on the belief that the newspaper could never become a "rising star" growth machine for Dow. This debased group defined their own success, they argued, as not allowing its core circulation to drop-down too fast. Thankfully, the corporate leadership did not allow that labeling to prevail.

To recap, Rich Zannino worked with the operating managers of *The Wall Street Journal* to clearly identify its core organic growth problems. He identified resources that were overlooked by *The Wall Street Journal's* management team. Working together they redeployed those key leveraged resources using them to solve the growth problems that had sent *The Wall Street Journal* into a downward spiral.

HOW TO BUILD BRIDGES FOR ORGANIC GROWTH TO OPERATING UNITS

The attentive Chief Growth Officer leads operating managers to look within, as well as outside of, operating units to make organic growth discoveries to transform the available resources into organic growth opportunities.

Building bridges requires you to take on an objective, high-level view. Look across entire businesses and vast markets to identify unique patterns. Bring this vantage point to operating units to form portfolio strategy.

Work with your operating unit manager until they can see around corners. Identify the highest and best opportunities. Most importantly, transform smaller opportunities into larger ones. For example, looking across operating units you might bring together small opportunities that make no sense by themselves, however, perhaps they can be bundled to create a big growth opportunity for the company.

In working with operating managers to make new growth discoveries, the Chief Growth Officer focuses on helping the operating unit manager in articulating the problem, developing a list of potential resources, identifying those resources that will have the most leverage in solving the organic growth problem, then employing these key catalyzing resources into amazing solutions.

CLEARLY ARTICULATE THE ORGANIC GROWTH PROBLEM OF THE OPERATING UNIT

The Chief Growth Officer uses clarifying questions, statements and probing inquiries to propel himself forward in identifying the core organic growth problem of the operating unit:

- What is the core organic growth problem of the operating unit?

- List any contributing causes or factors of the operating unit problem that will be the focus of your organic growth stimulation effort.

- What are the associated organizational outcome expectations of solving this problem?

- How well do the performance processes, management and initiatives align with the growth charter of the operating unit as laid out in the Growth Proposition? How do any misalignments affect performance?

- What underutilized resources and overlooked assets are not being used that could or should be employed to solve this problem, or create a new opportunity that would then solve this problem?

DEVELOP A LIST OF POTENTIAL RESOURCES FOR SOLVING THE PROBLEM

The Chief Growth Officer is actively working with operating managers in need of a boost. In keeping, the CGO will find it helpful to make a list of all internal and external resources at hand for the operating unit, leaving no stone unturned.

NARROW YOUR LIST TO IDENTIFY THE KEY RESOURCES YIELDING GREATEST GROWTH LEVERAGE

The key is to then narrow down the list of resources. Identify only those that have the leverage or potential to solve the problem and change the system of the operating unit without unwanted side effects. It is often in moments of sacred discussion that the Chief Growth Officer and unit manager can work together to discover revelations to better utilize resources, to make changes without creating drawbacks somewhere else.

Here are some examples:

Resource Conversion: Transform existing resources into new resources by applying inventive thinking, technology transfer, research, and field studies to the problem facing the operating unit manager. For example, Guinness saw bottled

Guinness as a growth opportunity in the Americas. However, bottled Guinness required a nitrogen capsule to be loaded into each bottle to accomplish this market growth. The Chief Executive Officer in cooperation with the operating unit manager had a special nitrogen capsule developed. The technology tested well in Ireland and in the United States, which justified the investment.

Resource Combination: Adding one resource to another to effect change. Ice cream was invented in 2000 B.C. Years later someone else created the ice cream cone, which revolutionized ice cream sales ever since.

Resource Evolution: Envisioning the evolution of a system involves looking at a growth challenge and asking: What resources, processes or systems might evolve and how? For example, when Mike Melio, of Western Piedmont Metal, Inc., wanted to increase growth in the number of customers his company serviced in the scrap metal business, he installed scales at each customer location. The scale provided a way to build trust with each potential client as a guaranteed upfront proof source showing what the metal was worth before it was hauled by his company. The result was over a 150%

growth in customer acquisition in the first year of implementing scales at Western Piedmont.

SOLVE THE ORGANIC GROWTH PROBLEM OF THE OPERATING UNIT

Several uses of resources could be deployed — teams of operating leaders could be organized to perform critical functions, resources could be used to mobilize and transport products to critical impact points that affect customers or suppliers. Other teams might create new leveraged product, service, marketing and/or selling solutions.

Interestingly, it turned out that for Guinness the bottled version of the product required extra changes to the distribution system in order to bring the bottled version of Guinness to market in the United States and Ireland.

For Western Piedmont Metal, transportation teams were mobilized to deliver scales for weighing scrap metal to customers on a roll-out schedule. Sales people were deployed with smart tablets to educate potential and existing customer accounts about the improvement in service.

For both Guinness and Western Piedmont Metal, the key growth leader was the willingness to look beyond the labels they had assigned to the operating units based on past performance. They found ways around the key problem by deploying resources that empowered the operating unit manager to deliver the highest possible growth leverage to the company.

CONCLUSION

Labeling operating divisions may cause operating managers and their teams to deliver results that are aligned with the associated expectation. This is a little bit similar to labeling one's children. "This is my eldest daughter, she is the go-getter. This is my middle child, he is my smart-dart, the sharpest kid in the neighborhood. Then there is my pretty little model in the corner over there." Why wouldn't we want to hold all three to an elevated performance target to see how far our expectations could lead them to achieve higher performance? Why not build a bridge instead?

It may turn out that the pretty model may have more potential than all of the others combined.

5

Make Funding Organic Growth Easier

Pushing for growth from the top of the organization is hard and often yields ineffective results because teams resist against the push. Pulling by incentivizing and empowering teams to grow is easier, and the results are often significantly better.

Before in-depth discussions about funding organic growth can take place, the growth-focused leader must be aware of what part of the business cycle the company is experiencing and how to maintain control over growth throughout the business cycle at all times, while being as objective as possible.

With a balanced perspective, the Chief Growth Officer understands the timing of key business cycle decisions. He is better able to work with operating unit managers to identify cost saving elements that can be used as investments in organic growth.

Furthermore, the introduction of a growth proposal program creates lively incentives for operating unit team members as they compete to provide operating unit managers with organic growth proposals teeming with new initiatives.

In this chapter, we will discuss each of these areas; maintaining control throughout the business cycle, identifying and reinvesting costs into organic growth, and using a growth proposal program to gain buy-in from motivated teams to implement organic growth initiatives.

MAINTAINING CONTROL THROUGHOUT THE BUSINESS CYCLE

For most companies, during the *boom* phase of the business cycle they invest aggressively in growth. In the *bust* phase, managers become cost conscious and focus on making cuts. By amplifying the cycle in this manner, corporate leaders can cause immeasurable harm to their operating units' organic growth efforts.

At the peak of the boom phase, this standard approach encourages operating unit managers to believe in overly optimistic business forecasts. After all, no one wants to be gloomy when business is going well. This makes it easy for managers to add unnecessary head count or to pay too much for an asset they believe they need.

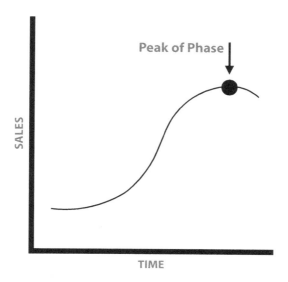

When the phase turns, they reverse course, at a significant cost in time, money and attention to growth.

At the bottom of the phase, cynical signals from corporate leaders can make operating unit managers hesitant to fund new products, upgrade customer service, or invest in marketing. The damage from such inaction often takes longer to materialize, but the impact is equally destructive.

Maintaining control by taking a strong leadership role throughout the business cycle takes gut-level resilience and

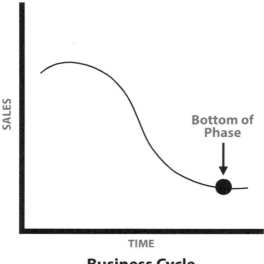

Business Cycle

fortitude. No one wants to discuss "growth investments" during a challenging time, or "steady measured growth" during a prosperous time.

Resisting firmly against the drumbeat of business phases is an essential role of the CGO, and this is one of the most important tests of executive resolve, especially for CEOs.

Furthermore, if the CGO faces resistance from the CEO or other corporate executives during the bottom phase of the business cycle, elevating the discussion to focus decisions about improving "relative customer value" can be useful. In addition, this topic can be helpful in reducing resistance from operating managers.

This does not mean the CGO should become countercyclical. Instead, the CGO must help lead the organization to invest in organic growth in a way that is independent of the business cycle.

Decisions made during an unexpected down-cycle must be considered carefully to ensure that funding for organic growth is considered, in the context of, yet separately from, the current sequence of external events. The key is to balance the external needs of the business with the need to maintain forward progress in organic growth.

TENACIOUSLY CONVERT COST SAVINGS INTO REINVESTMENTS IN ORGANIC GROWTH

Get on a mission. Go on a steadfast, persistent and single-minded hunt to cut out nonessential costs everywhere they can be found. Make a continual, brazen, invasive and pervasive effort to identify unnecessary overhead costs.

One way to make funding organic growth easier is with a zero-overhead growth approach to such decisions. With a zero-overhead growth approach, you work with operating unit managers to clearly identify non-essential costs. You cut the costs, and then reassign those cost savings as organic growth reinvestments back into the operating unit that achieved them, to benefit the initiative of the operating unit.

When CEO Jim Kilts realized that he needed to take the team at Gillette from denial that excess costs were an issue to acceptance of a zero-overhead approach to growth as a way of life, he led operating unit managers to begin to identify which costs could be eliminated, saved, and then reinvested to drive organic growth.

Cost discussions are never fun. But an incentive for cost cutting is a silver lining. When asking operating managers to remove overhead in order to take out costs that are no longer necessary, why not provide them with a reward — an incentive for doing so?

Every company must face short-term pressures in driving profit growth. This can be challenging when making investments in hiring positions, training people, advertising, developing new products, marketing more aggressively, or training a salesforce—all needed to grow the top line. All of these investments hit your bottom line before you receive the top-line benefit.

A challenge with organic growth is that the bulk of the investment is a P&L investment. Growth-focused corporate leaders think of the investment in organic growth as a Revenue Expenditure (REVEX), versus a Capital Expenditure (CAPEX). The organic growth investment hits the P&L immediately.

Allowing operating units to fund their own organic growth creates buy-in and gives them options to do something better. Giving operating units the option to reinvest their cost-savings fuels internal growth.

Kilts often tapered down the targets that his operating managers proposed. He reminded them that being the top one or two organization in a given year does not necessarily correlate with long-term industry leadership. His research determined that the quest to occupy those positions created a yo-yo or bounce effect. He reminded shareholders and his team that the winner over a five-year period is usually a company that has been in the top third for profitability and revenue growth each year.

His purpose was not to restrain the ambition of operating managers. Instead, his aim was to keep them from worrying about the wrong things at the wrong time. For example, he wanted to prevent them from obsessing about growth at the top of the business cycle then abandoning it at the bottom.

Kilts was incessant in removing unnecessary costs throughout all seasons of the business cycle. His objective of plowing much of the savings back in the operating units that had achieved them, continued to renew the unit's investment into organic growth. Because managers tend to slash a lot more overhead during lean times, this practice had the effect of boosting the operating units' growth initiatives when they would be otherwise least likely to invest in growth.

UNDERWRITE ORGANIC GROWTH WITH A GROWTH PROPOSAL PROGRAM

Kilts utilized the cost savings derived from using the zero-overhead approach to fund growth programs, which acted as corporate grants to operating units to fund growth initiatives.

For example, one unit manager made innovative reductions to the design and cost packaging of several of Gillette's razor models. Kilts rewarded the manager by moving the savings into the unit manager's "growth fund." The unit manager then utilized this former cost as a "found money" investment into the growth of the sales of the razor models. Over time the unit manager moved the razor product line from point A to point B on the below chart, thus transforming the cost savings of the razor packaging into an investment for sales growth. Zero-overhead growth can be attained through the adoption of a company-wide growth proposal program.

In my work with the corporate center of several companies, great efficiencies and benefits have been derived from the development of a growth proposal program as a way to award growth funding to an operating unit.

Zero Overhead Growth

There are three primary benefits to using a growth proposal program as the delivery mechanism for funding organic growth at the operating unit level:

- First, putting out an open call among team members requesting growth proposals to help solve certain growth challenges diffuses growth thinking throughout the organization with a true sense of ownership, value creation and possibility.

- Second, when developed and screened using cross-functional teams, growth proposals foster a high-level of buy-in toward the attainment of the overall growth goal of the company.

- Third, a growth proposal program fosters a sense of healthy competition by which the best ideas rise upward. A proper screening criteria and process is necessary to achieve positive results.

The use of an independent screening committee, or oversight board, is suggested to ensure the overall corporate growth goals are likely to be achieved with the selected growth proposals.

The program can stipulate that individual team members will receive an incentive for submitting a growth proposal, as well as when a proposal is selected for use in an operating unit. Such incentives can be based on monetary rewards, or recognition and award based, or a combination of each one.

The growth proposal program should be tied to the growth fund of each operating unit. The CGO should call for unit managers to contribute unit cost savings to their growth fund in alignment with the growth plans of the corporate center.

The growth proposal program demonstrates to unit managers that good ideas for increasing organic growth always find resources in the company, should be funded by zero-overhead cost reassignment whenever possible, and occur even at the bottom of the business cycle.

By providing structured incentives aimed at following zero-growth overhead cost restructuring, with growth briefs and proposals, the CGO will lead the corporate center to screen the unit managers' best-of-breed initiatives for funding approvals.

Clearly, earmarking operating unit local costs with a funding incentive that aligns with the overall growth goals of the corporate center makes it easier to fund organic growth.

6

Hone Your Organic Growth Process Model

Opportunities abound. Most companies' best growth opportunities lay hidden.

Overlooked opportunities lie dormant in the marketplace and remain unharvested because companies do not develop the tools and processes necessary to unearth them.

Opportunities lie in underutilized assets, such as well-performing marketing and advertising resources which are only taken so far by the firm, idle while these needs go unmet and unfulfilled.

Opportunities to mine sales hang in the company's customer base. Prospects remain in groups of previously captured, but yet unconverted customers. Then there are customers who have bought only introductory offerings but would buy more times if presented with the right offer or buying situation. Some would buy more often, if invited, under the right conditions. Some would purchase in a regular subscription-type of buying pattern when presented with the right offer.

Opportunities lie in the company's transaction vehicles. Some customers prefer to buy online on computers, some through smart phone apps, others in person, still others by telephone, some in their Xbox, and some by mail.

The list of opportunity pockets that are out in the world and inside of our businesses can be endless. Honing your organic growth process is about seeing what no one else in your company or industry sees. This means not only seeing the opportunity pockets that are available but having the ability to lead the company to unearth the right ones fully. This also means bringing the highest and best opportunities to transactional fruition by first driving the opportunities with the greatest potential to meet growth goals to their maximum monetary value equivalent.

As an enlightened corporate growth leader, you must make every waking effort to move toward an audacious target to grow faster than your fiercest competitor. You understand that in order to unearth, harvest and capture more opportunities than those competitors, you must create a system of innovative growth initiatives to fuel the top line while maintaining your version of zero-overhead, bottom-line growth.

For the CGO, it is important to build the growth model around the ideal cohesive set of initiatives and vehicles that best match the company's unique customers.

The growth-focused company views growth as a process. The growth process model is the structure of processes, the system of initiatives and metrics, that is defined and chosen by the CGO and corporate leaders to move the company in the direction of the growth target.

For large companies, a system of symbiotic acquisitions can serve the same purpose. I am drawing the distinction here that symbiotic acquisitions are not made for the sole sake of boosting organic growth, but rather to give the company important competencies necessary to take the company where it needs to go. Some companies do a lot of heavy lifting in their portfolios to get that synergistic juice. In this case, the acquisition becomes catalytic to the structure of initiatives in the company's growth model.

The growth process model must be developed and presented by the CGO as a clear diagram depicting how initiatives fit together to form the meta-organic growth process. I will give examples of growth process models below in this chapter, ranging from simple to complex.

The role of the CGO is to guide growth by leading transformative change. This objective has to be linked to hitting levers across all of the operating units—and it must keep that up over time. For multi-business companies, the levers are hit across all of the businesses. In order to hit targets, the meta-organic growth process becomes a valuable and necessary resource.

Internally, operating unit managers, customers, and investors all must see that the growth model is repeatable and working. This is the only way you get paid in the marketplace and increase the value of the company to each stakeholder over time.

Traditionally, most CEOs build out the core business over time, product line by product line, department by department, or division by division. Most never understand growth as a process.

In developing or evaluating the growth process model for clients, I suggest starting by identifying your highest and best growth factors, growth initiatives, support initiatives and structures that explain how each aspect of your growth process model supports a larger vision for organic growth.

Most of the CEOs who discovered the importance of focusing on growth as a process over a long period of time, have disclosed they would have preferred to work out a clear diagram of their growth process model early on, starting with a comprehensive approach.

SIMPLE X GROWTH PROCESS MODEL

In the Simple X Growth Process Model (following), growth is built on only three growth factors, which could be identifiable cross-sections or segments of the business. In the example given, the CGO focuses on setting direction, scope and targets for the cross-sections of the business. Operating unit managers deliver new initiatives to each cross-section. In the example below, the initiatives impact the growth factors of the number of customers and growth characteristics related to transactions, the value and the number of transactions.

In the following example, growth targets were set for each operating manager responsible for sales, marketing, promotion, and product development.

An increase in advertising inventories and media buying was ordered and set into the budget. The operating managers for the sales, marketing and CRM teams developed new initiatives and growth proposals requested by corporate leaders for jump-starting lead generation. Two were selected. Sales managers signed contracts with non-competitive suppliers down-channel to refer new clients to the company and incentives were provided.

Furthermore, the sales manager, product development director and marketing survey research leader worked on a cross-functional team to produce growth proposals

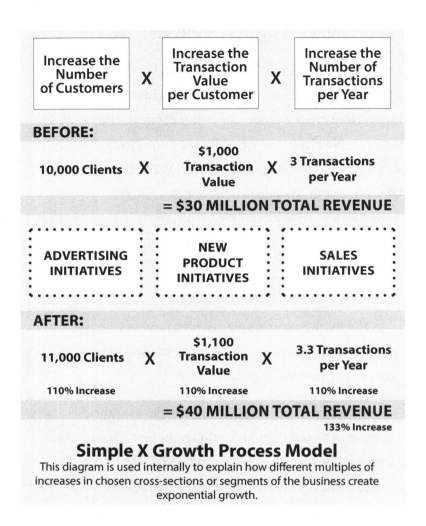

Increase the Number of Customers	X	Increase the Transaction Value per Customer	X	Increase the Number of Transactions per Year

BEFORE:

10,000 Clients	X	$1,000 Transaction Value	X	3 Transactions per Year

= $30 MILLION TOTAL REVENUE

ADVERTISING INITIATIVES	NEW PRODUCT INITIATIVES	SALES INITIATIVES

AFTER:

11,000 Clients	X	$1,100 Transaction Value	X	3.3 Transactions per Year
110% Increase		110% Increase		110% Increase

= $40 MILLION TOTAL REVENUE

133% Increase

Simple X Growth Process Model
This diagram is used internally to explain how different multiples of increases in chosen cross-sections or segments of the business create exponential growth.

focused on new product development. The marketing manager implemented a plan to add the products to the customer journey through sales staff offers and through the company's online buying experience.

Finally, a special team was developed to spearhead special online and offline customer events through live webinars, trade shows and local retail establishments.

At each juncture, the initiatives came together to bring more customers into buying situations, and give incentives for receiving extra value for buying. Upon purchase, customers were offered additional incentives for upgrading to more advanced versions of the offerings selected. In addition, customers were provided with the option of adding newly-developed, innovative products at the point of purchase.

Results were analyzed in real-time throughout the year and appropriate changes were made to products, programs and selling environments to optimize the customer experience and exceed the growth targets.

MULTI-PART GROWTH PROCESS MODEL

In the Multi-Part Growth Process (following), which is similar to the one General Electric has used successfully, growth is built on six traits (i.e. Imagination Breakthroughs), six growth factors (i.e. Globalization) with growth initiatives and support structures.

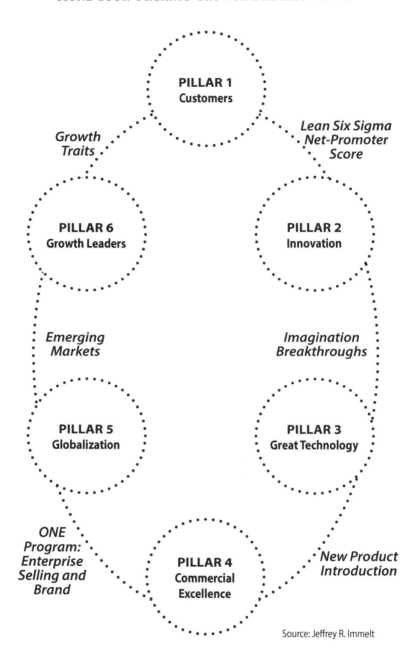

Multi-Part Growth Process

In this model, growth is achieved by using strategic symbiotic acquisitions to increase integrative competencies with best-of-breed initiatives. Larger organizations running multi-business companies benefit greatly from utilizing the growth proposal process, as described in the previous chapter, in order to develop initiatives that are identified, screened and selected by the corporate center.

As one example, referral initiatives were introduced by operating unit managers and the net promoter score was used company-wide to support referral-based program initiatives. The net promoter score measures the willingness of the customer to recommend a company's products or services to others.

Here we see there are at most six important pillars upon which the Multi-Part Growth Process Model is built with six important supporting traits, which together provide a growth synergy to the business. The number of pillars used by organizations adopting the Multi-Part Growth Process Model will vary depending on the size and scope of the organization.

The CGO, in cooperation with the corporate center, must identify the right base factors, growth factors, growth initiatives, support initiatives and structures for the pillars selected. It is from this integrated system of processes that operating unit managers will launch plans and hit targets.

Every corporate growth leader will create a different and unique growth process model that is right for their company, based on the values, culture, industry, structure of the core business, and type of customers and markets served. Of course, there are many other nuances and factors for a myriad of different businesses that must be considered, are too numerous to name and are well beyond the scope of this book.

FUNNEL-ASCENSION GROWTH PROCESS MODEL

In the Funnel-Ascension Growth Process Model (opposite), the job of the CGO is to orchestrate growth across the entire business. The growth targets are reached by taking customers through a buying process and then ascending them to higher levels of purchase over time.

The Funnel-Ascension Growth Process Model works well with companies using direct and indirect customer selling and distribution channels, traditional sales-focused organizations and technology-driven marketing companies. This model works particularly well when team talent, technology and content are both outstanding and abundant throughout the company.

The CGO uses this model to explain and orchestrate how growth is accomplished as customers move through the business. Initiatives are orchestrated as the volume of

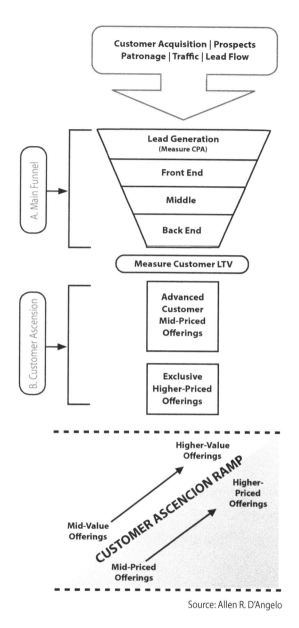

Source: Allen R. D'Angelo

Funnel-Ascension Growth Process Model

This diagram is used internally to explain how to grow the business as customers move through the business.

customers and the value of customers increase as they move upward along the Customer Ascension Ramp simultaneously.

Rovi Entertainment, creator of Angry Birds, used the Funnel-Ascension Growth Process Model by applying gamification to their direct and indirect channel market approach. The model spanned across multiple platforms and media to create a preeminent brand with its app game characters.

You may recall that the customers of Rovi Entertainment first entered the top of their Funnel-Ascension Growth Process Model by downloading a free version of the Angry Birds app to their smart phones. The offering was followed by a 99¢ version of the Angry Birds app. Low-cost app downloads are perceived as relatively low-risk activities by consumers. The widespread instant deliverability of smart phones was paired with a pleasurable gaming experience. The result for Rovi Entertainment was a giant tidal wave of prospects into the top of their funnel.

Four years after introducing the Angry Birds app, customers responded quite favorably as Rovi Entertainment recorded over 2 billion downloads of this app across all platforms.

Once customers completed game play of the cheaper and easier version of the app and were hooked on playing the game, they were offered advanced versions.

As players entered the world of the game and engagement deepened, they bonded with the characters. As players conquered progressively higher levels of game play they became empowered heroes of the game as they were rewarded. Based on their scores, they received either high-fives or dirty glares from friends or family members; this contributed to a stimulating and pleasurable experience for many.

As consumers traveled into the front-end, middle and back-end of the funnel, Rovi Entertainment offered them PC games, console gaming, merchandising and movie licensing, which drove growth for the company on the back-end as well as through the customer ascension process. Advanced customer ascension occurred as Angry Birds diffused the culture. Through Rovi Entertainment's licensing relationships with food products, toys, film, television, print publication and other adaptations, consumers ascended to higher purchase levels.

One of the best examples of Rovi Entertainment's application of the Funnel-Ascension Growth Process Model in play came to life before me through a neighborhood friend. Her name is Celeste and her family loved Angry Birds. While socializing with the family, I saw their collection of Angry Birds products grow within months. There were Angry Birds plush pillows, books, action-figures, and other collectibles. For their child's birthday, they ordered a fully decorated Angry Birds birthday cake.

The quick math I calculated at the time put this raving fan family at approximately $300+, based on a one-year lifetime value for the Angry Birds brand as they reached the top of the customer ascension ramp.

GROWTH PROCESS MODEL STACKING

Over the course of the past ten years in my work with clients, I have built Growth Process Models, expanded and renovated them, as well as added and stacked them together in special situations.

Once the core Growth Process Model has been identified and the corporate growth executives and operating managers are adept at scaling the business, it can be useful to stack new and different Growth Process Models as sub-models into the core business. Simple X Models can be stacked into key portions of a company's Funnel-Ascension Growth Process Model in more than one area to achieve extra double-digit growth with, at times, minimal re-investment or change to the structures of the business.

ON GROWTH HACKING

Growth Process Model Stacking is not the same as the commonly used term, "growth hacking," which has become a popular term, especially amid technology and other more entrepreneurial companies, such as those receiving angel investment.

Growth hacking utilizes speedy experimentation whereby experts, marketing channel managers, creative leaders and product development people pinpoint the most efficient ways to grow an operating unit.

For smaller companies, some form of growth hacking is often used in and across operating units as cross-functional teams come together to solve a problem. As an example, marketers, engineers and product managers may unite to determine why a product has a low number of user trials and to work together to generate a hacked solution; to find a creative way to accomplish growth using innovation from each of their discipline areas. The CGO should harness growth hacking applications and must never allow them to undermine, or derail, the direction set by the corporate center.

The corporate center should approve all activities as they contribute best to the accomplishment of the core growth proposition of the company. In addition, all proposed growth initiatives must fit snugly within the core Growth Process Model that is agreed upon by the corporate center and unit operating managers.

7

Balance Margin and Growth

One important question elevates the discussion about decisions affected by growth and margin. The crux of the question focuses on where the real potential value generation lies for shareholders, in the case of publicly held companies, and owners and investors, for privately held businesses. The issue usually arises around how decisions are made about attaining extra growth versus acquiring margin.

This is the question: "Which is more valuable to your company, achieving an additional percentage point of growth, or adding an extra percentage point of margin?"

At the outset, an extra point of margin looks significantly more valuable because, as many CFOs argue, 100% of the extra margin falls to the bottom line. While most agree, perhaps only 7% to 8% of an extra point of growth turns into profit. This only happens if the profit margin is sustained.

At the same time, corporate growth officers with experience know that growth has a compounding effect, which over time amplifies the long-term benefit.

Many executives have argued that a point of growth and a point of margin probably contributed equally to shareholder value. And yet, countless experienced business leaders do not have a clear sense of the relative impact that growth and extra margin have on their shareholder value.

Experience and empirical research has confirmed time and again that growth and margin are not always equal.

The value of attained growth is quite often far greater than the operating manager may first realize. It is an error to assume that profitability must be surrendered to achieve growth, although there are particular situations where it does. This is why the diligent CGO should introduce innovative, new, zero-overhead organic growth thinking to operating unit managers during strategic meetings.

For some companies, convincing the team that growth by only one additional percentage point may be worth seven, or eight, or perhaps ten or more points of extra margin, is a challenge.

The choice of whether to adopt a margin increase or a growth strategy is rarely obvious, and hinges on factors related to the specific company situation as well as key industry dynamics.

Some companies regularly under weigh the value of growth and, in keeping, jeopardize the company's performance and sustainability. Others power-up growth engines when shareholder value would be better served by jump-starting margins and cash flow. Some doggedly fight the battles of seasons past by staying with outdated and outmoded approaches far longer than they should.

The CGO works with operating managers in aligning the resources and energies of the operating units across growth initiatives and margin improvement initiatives to reach growth targets. At certain times, the CGO will decide to use relative value of growth (RVG) as a tool to think differently about key operating decisions.

As we will see below, RVG can be instrumental in many situations in stimulating new ideas about more ways for making growth free to the organization.

For many years in business, there has been an unspoken notion amidst some leaders that profitability and growth are incompatible in the long term. While it is beyond the scope of this chapter to address this issue, many companies are effective at delivering both. Furthermore, it is the role of corporate growth leaders to deliver on both profitability and growth.

In-depth analysis of the relative value of growth metric framework reveals that companies benefit more, as far as stock price goes, from giving the market reason to expect extra growth than from improving cost structures.

Corporate growth leaders who develop a sound framework for applying relative value of growth measures to their businesses will define strategies that enable them to better balance growth and profitability at the corporate and operating unit level.

The experienced corporate growth leader understands the value of measuring the RVG of their organization. The below Relative Value of Growth (RVG) Framework provides the steps the CGO should use to determine the RVG measure of the company.

An RVG of 6.2 tells the CGO that one extra point of growth yields as much value as 6.2 extra points of margin.

Calculating RVGs gives corporate leaders insights into which corporate strategies are working to deliver value. When comparing the RVG of different companies in a sector or industry, RVG reveals whether or not companies are pulling the most powerful levers for value creation.

A few years ago, after reading research by investment banker Nathanial Mass, I studied RVG calculations for Procter and Gamble (P&G). The company's RVG was 7.2. This tell us that if P&G were to improve the company's margin by just a single point, the result would be about $7.35 billion in added shareholder value—a solid jump up of nearly 5% to total enterprise value. However, if management could convince the market to expect an extra point of revenue growth from P&G, the company would create more than $52 billion in added shareholder value—boosting current enterprise value by a full 34%. The RVG of 7.2 revealed that the company would have to squeeze out 7.2 points of additional operating margin (giving the company an operating margin at the time of 25%) in order to deliver the benefits of just one more point of growth. For P&G, raising margin would constitute a large, if not impossible, challenge to execute. In this case, delivering value through raising growth expectations is clearly the easier option.

For operating decisions, strategy is not about making an either/or decision about whether to grow or concentrate on margins. Growth and margin are not necessarily mutually exclusive to one another. To create the most value operationally, leaders must define more agile and ambitious strategies to strike the proper balance between cost control and revenue growth, such as by using zero overhead growth.

The decisions emanating from the corporate center should support the CGO in achieving this balance.

Corporate growth leaders will find relative value of growth to be a tool to stimulate conversations and decisions about cost management and revenue growth at the product level.

For one company, the product-related operating units were stuck in "maintenance mode," for example, with high support costs, slowing down the flow of new products to new and existing markets. By thinking differently, using an innovative zero-overhead approach to growth, research and development costs were shifted, including the cost of supporting the product's online ticketing system. This freed up revenue to put the commercialization of new products on the fast track.

The enlightened CGO will use many varied skills and tools to balance growth and margin decisions to keep growth, profits, cash flow and the company as a whole moving forward.

RVG can be a powerful instrument. When used properly, it brings thought-leadership to the table as the CGO opens up new avenues of thinking about finding new ways to make growth free to the organization.

The Relative Value of Growth (RVG) Framework

This framework provides corporate growth leaders and operating unit managers with a clear understanding of the relative impact of growth and additional margin on shareholder value for relevant strategic decision making. The RVG tool measures the relative value of growth (RVG) for the company—comparisons can be made to competitors. The RVG measures the extent to which one more percentage point of growth impacts shareholder value compared with addtional point of margin.

Step 1: Weighted Average Cost of Capital
Calculate the company's weighted average cost of capital:

Cost of Debt x (1- tax rate) x Debt Ratio + (Cost of Equity x Equity Ratio)

Step 2: Discounted Cash Flow Model
Build a fundamental growth model, in perpetuity, to determine shareholders' average growth expectation over time.

$$EV = \frac{CF}{WACC - g} \qquad g = Expected\ Rate\ of\ Growth$$

Step 3: Calculate The Value of Margin Improvement
Calculate the value of a 1% improvement to operating margin on revenues (adjust for your corporate tax rate).

Increase in Cash Flow (ICF) = Revenues x (1%) x (1-35%)

$$Value\ of\ Margin\ Improvement = \frac{ICF}{10\% - (g)}$$

Step 4: Relative Value of Growth
Calculate to compare the relative value of growth with the value of margin improvement.

RVG = Value of Growth + Value of Margin Improvement

$$\frac{Value\ of\ Growth}{Value\ of\ Margin\ Improvement} = RVG$$

Source: Nathaniel J. Mass

103

The Relative Value of Growth (RVG) Framework Example

Corporate Data:

Enterprise Value (EV) = $1B
Market Cap = $700M
Debt = $300M
Debt-to-Equity Ratio = 3.7
Revenues = $400M

EBIT = $68M
Cash Flow (CF) = $40M
Cost of Equity = 12.5%
Cost of Debt = 6%

Step 1: Weighted Average Cost of Capital

Calculate the company's weighted average cost of capital:

Cost of Debt x (1- tax rate) x debt ratio + (cost of equity x equity ratio)

Step 2: Discounted Cash Flow Model

Build a fundamental growth model, in perpetuity, to determine shareholders' average growth expectation over time.

$$EV = \frac{CF}{WACC - g} \qquad g = Expected\ Rate\ of\ Growth$$

Step 3: Calculate Expected Growth

Use fundamental algebra to solve for *g*

$$\$1B = \frac{\$40M}{10\% - g} \qquad g = 6\%$$

Step 4: Calculate The Value of Growth

Calculate the value of one additional percentage point of growth using the valuation model from above step 2.

$$\$18 = \frac{\$40M}{10\% - (6\%+1\%)} \qquad Value\ of\ Growth = \$333M$$

Step 5: Calculate The Value of Margin Improvement

Calculate the value of a 1% operating margin improvement on revenues of $400M (adjusted for corporate tax rate).

Increase in Cash Flow = $400M x (1%) x (1-35%) = $2.6M

$$Value\ of\ Margin\ Improvement = \frac{\$2.6M}{10\% - (6\%)} = \$65M$$

Step 6: Relative Value of Growth

Determine the relative value of growth.

RVG = Value of Growth + Value of Margin Improvement

$$\frac{\$333M}{\$65M} = 5.1 \qquad RVG = 5.1$$

Source: Nathaniel J. Mass

Epilogue

In this book, I have shared seven key principles, one per chapter, as derived and codified from my collective work in the field with clients. I have attempted to distill my body of research, applied knowledge and initiatives down to a cogent set of practical organic growth precepts for direct application by growth-focused leaders from organizations of all sizes.

Over two decades of research and experiments have guided the discovery and development of the principles presented throughout this book.

My goal in writing this book has been to provide a strong framework for tackling perplexing problems associated with organic growth issues in this modern age fraught with disruptive influences.

As you apply the principles in each of the chapters of this book to your business endeavors I wish the following for you:

> Under your leadership, may your teams be perpetually inspired by the brilliance of your articulation of the company's vision for growth.

> May your growth vision be one that is so clearly understood and loved by every person at each level in your company, that word of it diffuses and spreads out from your company like wildfire across a barren land.

> May you be perpetually empowered to gently, but diligently tear down any limiting walls, siloes, and barriers you encounter, and do so wherever you find them.

> May you find resourceful new ways to make funding growth fun and free, even if that means disrupting the status quo of your company or industry.

> May you always find the balance between growth and margin. And when you cannot, my hope is for you to always land on the right side of this fence for all the right reasons.

Above all, my wish for you—my dear growth-focused executive—is that you remain true to yourself and your vision at all times.

Return to this book whenever you need a gentle reminder to apply the principles of organic organizational growth to your situation at hand. Come back to the 'Organic Growth Assessment Questions for Corporate Leaders' Appendix often to check-up and check-in on your application of all of the principles of *The Chief Growth Officer's Manifesto*.

I wish you well in all of your endeavors. All my best to you!

Allen R. D'Angelo M.S.

Fellow Chief Growth Officer

Appendix

Organic Growth
Assessment for
Corporate Leaders

The ability of the company to create organic growth depends a lot on the leadership team of the company. Read through the below questions, which are focused on the seven key disciplines of the *The Chief Growth Officer Manifesto*. If you cannot answer *yes* to at least five of the questions in each below discipline area, your company may not be reaching its organic growth potential.

How good is leadership at sharing the vision for the big picture with the organization?

☐ Do we maintain a carefully crafted written core growth proposition that is available to all employees of the company to understand?

☐ Do we maintain a database of company-wide organic growth ideas and opportunities that everyone may contribute to?

☐ Do we maintain a written detailed criterion for the size and scope of the organic growth ideas we want to unearth?

☐ Do we look for more than "low hanging fruit" or "shallow pool" organic growth opportunities 80% of the time?

☐ Is the CEO active in connecting organic growth plays of operating units to the vision of the company?

☐ Does the corporate team look across operating units to find opportunities that no unit can see or pursue on its own?

☐ Does our company have unique capabilities that enable operating units to achieve more organic growth than our competitors?

How good is leadership at creating formal structures for communicating about organic growth throughout the organization?

☐ Do we use a common growth language across the entire company?

☐ Do we have a clear definition of "organic growth opportunity?"

☐ Does each of the important growth terms that are discussed in your company relate to a measurable company target?

☐ Do we proactively measure the *relative customer value* of new initiatives in the company?

☐ Do we have a formal organic glossary of growth language terms and have we disseminated the glossary in writing to everyone in the company?

☐ Do the questions the CEO poses to key leaders in the company assist each operating unit in identifying its growth opportunities and deciding how to best realize them?

☐ Do all leaders in the company tend to accurately estimate growth potential consistently?

Do we successfully clarify our growth targets?

☐ Are all of our operating units successfully meeting growth targets?

☐ Is one or more of our operating units being driven harder by leadership than others or exceeding growth targets more noticeably compared to others?

☐ Are all of our operating units meeting growth targets each quarter?

☐ Do we regularly measure the natural growth rates for the markets we compete in?

☐ Do we have a clarified and objective picture of the actual headroom for growth our company has available?

☐ Are there ever any holdbacks or reservations on the part of leadership throughout a year when it is time to make investments in growth?

☐ Do we engage an outside growth consultant to provide an objective assessment of our growth targets each quarter?

Is our current portfolio strategy effectively contributing to growth?

☐ Does our company avoid labels such as "cash cow" or "rising star?"

☐ Do we require operating units to find new ways to boost organic growth?

☐ Do we require operating units to fund organic growth?

☐ Are all operating managers diligently seeking advancements and innovations?

☐ Does technology play a role in our growth strategy?

☐ Do we require operating units to squeeze out more profits in order to fund their growth initiatives?

☐ Are we hiring next-level management for higher-performing operating units?

Do we have an effective and sustainable growth funding strategy?

☐ Do we invest more in growth during the boom phase of a business cycle?

☐ Are we hesitant to fund growth during the down phase of the business cycle?

☐ Do we sometimes face resistance from other leaders about funding growth?

☐ Do we allow operating units to fund their own growth?

☐ Do we ever taper down targets that our operating managers propose?

☐ Do we use a growth proposal process to stimulate new growth ideas and to fund our growth?

☐ Do local operating units constantly generate cost savings in order to fund our organic growth?

Do we have a formal organic growth process in place?

☐ Do we give operating units the right performance standards for the long run?

☐ Have we identified a formal organic growth process with a complete diagram depicting the dynamics of our growth process model?

☐ Have we developed an organized system of initiatives and metrics for driving growth that everyone in the company can see and understand?

☐ Do we have a formal list of target companies for a symbiotic acquisition that would move the company closer to its growth target faster?

☐ Do we currently use a defined organic growth process to provide certainty of reaching our targets?

☐ Is our current organic growth process repeatable and working?

☐ Is our current process capable of delivering exponential growth?

Are we balancing decision making by considering growth and margin issues?

☐ Does our company have a clear sense of the relative impact that growth and extra margin have on shareholder value?

☐ Do our leaders tend to believe, in most situations, that profitability must be surrendered to achieve growth?

☐ Does our company tend to under-weigh the value of growth in important decisions?

☐ Do we have tools readily at hand for stimulating new ideas about more ways for making growth free to the company?

☐ Do we use the concept of relative value of growth to raise or support cost management initiatives?

☐ Do we as a company regularly free up revenue by using innovative zero-overhead growth thinking to reallocate costs and to put the commercialization of new programs and initiatives on the fast track?

☐ Has our company found the perfect balance between cost control and growing revenues?

References

Accenture, Inc. (November 2016). *CMOs First in the Firing Line If Business Growth Targets Are Not Met, Accenture Strategy Study Finds.* In-house Press Release.

Baghai, M., et. al. (May 2009). *Is Your Growth Strategy Flying Blind.* Harv Bus Rev.

Berry, Leonard (1999). *Discovering the Soul of Service: The Nine Drivers of Sustainable Business Success,* Free Press.

Favaro, K. et. al. (May 2012). *Creating an Organic Growth Machine.* Harv Bus Rev.

Harbison, J.R. et. al. (2016). *Making Acquisitions Work: Capturing Value After the Deal.* Booz-Allen & Hamilton Inc.

Immelt, J. (June 2006). *Growth as a Process.* Harv Bus Rev.

Kilts, James, M. (2007). *Doing What Matters: How to Get Results That Make a Difference—The Revolutionary Old-School Approach.* New York: Random House.Is

Mass, N.J. (April 2005). *The Relative Value of Growth.* Harv Bus Rev.

Resources from the Author

Additional *Chief Growth Officer Manifesto* resource materials are available through our education center, including the **Growth Core Competency Scorecard.** If you are an officer or business leader of a privately held company in a decision-making capacity, or a leader in an Inc. 5000 or a Fortune 5000 company, measure your progress across the Seven Growth Core Competencies by visiting: www.cgomanifesto.com.

Index